VIOLIN/EASY VIOLIN

Traditional fiddle music from around the world

EARLY MUSIC FIDDLER

Selected and arranged by
Edward Huws Jones

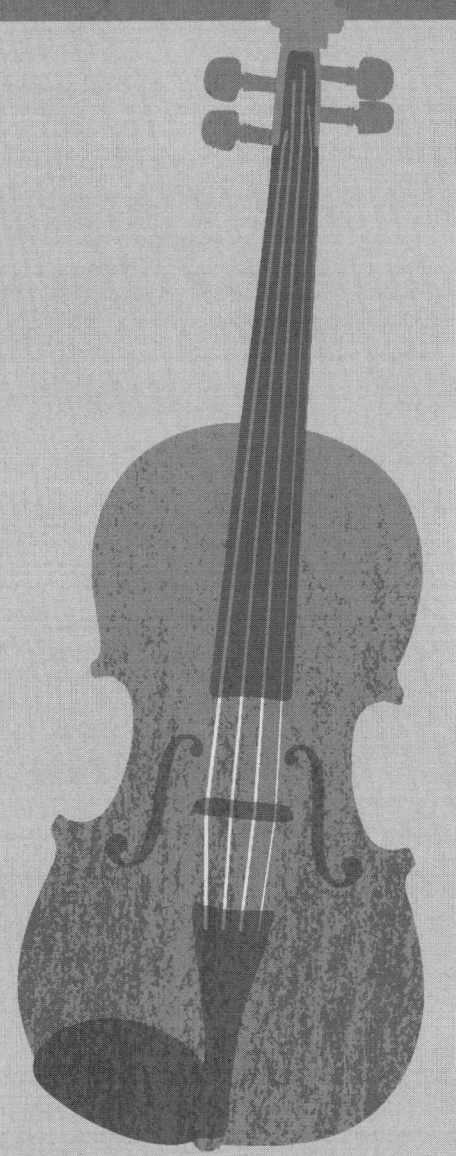

BOOSEY & HAWKES

Published by Boosey & Hawkes Music Publishers Ltd
Aldwych House
71–91 Aldwych
London
WC2B 4HN

www.boosey.com

© Copyright 2000 by Boosey & Hawkes Music Publishers Ltd
New edition © Copyright 2024 by Boosey & Hawkes Music Publishers Ltd

ISMN 979-0-060-11217-1 | ISBN 978-0-85162-277-4 (complete)
ISMN 979-0-060-11218-8 | ISBN 978-0-85162-278-1 (separately sold violin part)

Printed by Halstan:
Halstan UK, 2-10 Plantation Road, Amersham, Bucks, HP6 6HJ. United Kingdom
Halstan DE, Weißliliengasse 4, 55116 Mainz. Germany

Music setting by Jack Thompson

Cover design by Chloë Alexander Design
Cover image: Paul Hughes

EARLY MUSIC FIDDLER

Selected and arranged by
Edward Huws Jones

Preface and performance notes iv

MEDIEVAL SONGS AND DANCES

English dance	*13th century English*	2
Estampie royale	*13th century French*	4
L'homme armé	*15th century French*	6
Winder wie ist	*Neithart von Reuenthal*	7
Saltarello	*14th century Italian*	8

MUSIC AT COURT

J'ay mis mon cuer	*Guillaume Dufay*	10
Par le regard de vos beaux yeux	*Guillaume Dufay*	11
Pastime with good company	*atrrib. Henry VIII*	12
Hélas madame	*atrrib. Henry VIII*	13
Recercada	*Diego Ortiz*	14

RENAISSANCE POPULAR MUSIC

Ach Els'lein, liebstes Elselein	*15th century German*	16
La gamba	*16th century Italian*	17
Calata	*16th century Italian*	18
Kemp's jig	*16th century English*	20
Watkins' ale	*16th century English*	21

THE RENAISSANCE DANCE-BAND

Ronde: Pour quoy	*Tielman Susato*	22
La morisque	*Tielman Susato*	22
Pavane: La Venissienne	*Claude Gervaise*	24
La bouree	*Michael Praetorius*	25
Gaillarde: Mrs Winter's jump	*Michael Praetorius*	26

Preface

Here is a collection which spans four centuries and more than five countries - some vibrant threads from the rich tapestry of early music.

I first became enthralled by early music in the 1970s. It was an exhilarating time, with musicians like David Munrow and Anthony Rooley rediscovering whole worlds of medieval and renaissance music and bringing it to life in performance. Now this repertoire is well established, and we are seeing fresh approaches to it. Today Jan Garbarek and the Hilliard Ensemble tour the world playing a blend of medieval polyphony and jazz saxophone; CDs of Gregorian chant and the works of Hildegard of Bingen are best-sellers. Early music is off its pedestal and integrated into the everyday world!

We don't necessarily think of the violin as an early music instrument but in fact it evolved soon after 1500, during the early years of the musical renaissance, in a form more or less as we know it today. Most of the music in this anthology has some connection with stringed instruments, either the violin itself or one of its forerunners such as the rebec, medieval fiddle or viol. Significantly, all the pieces seem totally at home on the violin - and of course the player's own vitality and enthusiasm are far more important than strict historical accuracy.

The arrangements in this collection follow the same flexible format as other books in the series, and can be performed as solos, duets, or trios or by larger ensembles. Violin accompaniments for the more advanced player are given at the end of the complete book. The piano accompaniments can be played on a variety of keyboard instruments. Harpsichord or organ - or similar sounds on an electronic keyboard - work well, particularly in the renaissance pieces. All the earlier, medieval pieces have come down to us as a single melodic line, so the accompaniments have been freely arranged, usually based on ostinati. But the tunes can work just as well with the players adding their own drones and/or percussion. With the later tunes, we know that renaissance musicians loved to improvise variations or 'divisions' on well-known tunes. Some are suggested here, but performers are always encouraged to create their own!

My thanks to John Bryan and the York Early Music Festival; to Polly Waterfield for her insights into both early music and violin teaching; to Anthony Marks for helping to make sure the tapestry never came unravelled; and, above all, to all those musicians with whom I have at various times travelled through Europe with strangely-shaped instrument cases, playing lutes, viols, rebecs and fiddles.

Edward Huws Jones

Performance notes

English dance This sizzler of a tune is something of a one-off - no comparable dance music has survived from medieval England. The first half of the tune has a clear pattern shape; then it takes off, more in the manner of an improvisation. If you want to play a shorter version, stop at bar 24. A literal transcription of the original is in Davison and Apel, *Historical Anthology of Music* (1946).

Estampie royale Most medieval dances are of a type known as the estampie. An estampie consists of a string of short sections. Each one is played twice, with the same alternate endings repeated throughout the piece. This one is from a collection of French estampies from the 13th century. These dances have to be fast: listen to the hot performance by David Munrow and James Blades on *Music of the Crusades*.

L'homme armé ("The man at arms") This French folk song is one of the most famous of all medieval melodies. The words translate roughly as "Beware of the man at arms: you are going to need iron armour!". The performance needs to be suitably rhythmic and boisterous.

Winder wie ist ("Winter has gone") Neithart von Reuenthal was a minnesinger - the German equivalent of a troubadour. This song celebrates the coming of May and the end of winter. The tune is usually given in 4/4 but this 6/8 version brings out its lively, bouncy quality.

Saltarello This piece is from an Italian manuscript of the 14th century, now held in the British Library. *Saltarello* has a real folk-fiddle quality, with its open fifths and irrepressibly jig-like rhythm.

J'ay mis mon cuer ("I placed my heart") The lyrics may be about love, but the music needs to be assertive and rhythmic. Our version takes only the first half of Dufay's original 3-part song. The keyboard part is loosely based on the two lower voices. Exciting performances of this and the following piece can be heard on Ensemble Unicorn's *Dufay: Chansons*.

Par le regard de vos beaux yeux ("At the sight of your beautiful eyes") This was one of Dufay's most popular works - it is found in no fewer than 14 contemporary manuscripts. The words of the title say it all. In performance it needs to be tender and lyrical. Dufay's two lower parts are given as the second violin and violin accompaniment, so three violins can play the piece in its original form.

Pastime with good company Henry VIII of England was a keen amateur musician. This and the following melody come from a manuscript compiled at court during the earlier part of his reign. The piece lends itself to ornamentation and it can be embellished in any number of ways to suit the imagination and skill of the players.

Hélas madame ("Alas, Madam") This is another song from the court of Henry VIII. The French words are rather plaintive, but the music is high-spirited and boisterous!

Recercada Diego Ortiz was a Spanish viol player and his *Tratado de Glosas* (1553) was a kind of teach-yourself guide to composing divisions (ornamental variations). Recercada means to seek out - to explore the possibilities in a musical theme or idea. This recercada is quite playful in character, rather like a delightful musical doodle. Enjoy the off-beat minims and dotted crotchets.

Ach Els'lein, liebstes Elselein ("Oh Caroline, beloved Caroline") This poignant folk song was a great favourite with German composers of the Renaissance. This setting is based on the version in the *Glogauer Liederbuch*.

La gamba This melody and its underlying chord sequence were often used as a framework for divisions - Ortiz gives two different versions. In England it was even given words - "Blame not my Lute" - by Sir Thomas Wyatt.

Calata This has always been one of my favourite tunes, with all the inspired spontaneity of authentic folk music. The melody, with its jaunty, almost swaggering lilt, is adapted here from the 16th-century lute tablature.

Kemp's jig I first learnt this tune from a recording by a 1970s folk-rock band called Gryphon. The version here is based on a 16th-century English lute tablature. It is an archetypal Elizabethan dance tune with an exuberant two-in-a-bar feel.

Watkins' ale This delightful, rather cheeky melody and its accompanying variations are adapted from versions in the *Fitzwilliam Virginal Book* and the *Welde Lute Book*. The variations are optional - if you prefer, just repeat lines 1, 3 and 5.

Ronde: Pour quoy Susato was not so much a composer as an arranger and publisher. His four-part dances don't specify instrumentation, but this graceful melody is ideally suited to the violin. In all these dance pieces it is important to vary the articulation: it is often effective to play step-wise movement fairly legato and bigger intervals or repeated notes more detached.

La morisque This is a lively, uncomplicated Morris-dance tune in a rollicking duple pulse.

Pavane: La Venissienne This piece is built on an immensely popular bass line known as the passamezzo antico - the same bass, in fact, as is found in *Greensleeves*. The pavane has a processional quality, stately but not too slow.

La bouree Praetorius's *Terpsichore* (1612) is a vast anthology of dance music, most of which dates back to the previous century. *La Bouree* needs a strong two-in-a-bar pulse to bring out the rather comical rhythmic patterns.

Gaillarde: Mrs Winter's jump Praetorius calls this simply *Gaillarde* but it is in fact an arrangement of a popular Elizabethan melody. The title tells us exactly how to play it!

Préface

Ceci est un recueil qui couvre une période de quatre siècles dans plus de cinq pays – images vibrantes de la riche tapisserie de la musique ancienne.

Je fus séduit pour la première fois par la musique ancienne dans les années 1970. C'était une période enivrante : des musiciens tels que David Munrow et Anthony Rooley redécouvraient la musique médiévale et celle de la Renaissance et leur redonnaient vie en les jouant en public. Ce répertoire est maintenant bien établi et nous voyons de nouvelles approches se développer. Aujourd'hui Jan Garbarek et le Hilliard Ensemble font le tour du monde : leurs concerts mêlent polyphonie médiévale et saxophone de jazz ; les CD de chants grégoriens et les œuvres d'Hildegard von Bingen se vendent comme des petits pains. La musique ancienne est descendue de son piédestal et s'est intégrée à la vie de tous les jours !

En général le violon n'est pas considéré comme un instrument de musique ancienne mais en réalité il est apparu peu après l'an 1500, au début de la Renaissance musicale, sous une forme qui est plus ou moins celle que nous lui connaissons aujourd'hui. La plupart des œuvres de cette anthologie ont un lien avec les instruments à corde, qu'il s'agisse du violon lui-même ou de l'un de ses prédécesseurs tels que le rebec, le violon médiéval ou la viole. Il est révélateur que tous les morceaux sont parfaitement adaptés au violon, et bien sûr la vitalité et l'enthousiasme du musicien lui-même sont plus importants que la précision historique.

Les arrangements de ce recueil suivent le même format souple que dans les autres livres de la série et peuvent être joués en solo, en duo ou en trio, ou par des ensembles plus grands. Les accompagnements pour violon, pour les musiciens les plus expérimentés, sont donnés à la fin du livre. Les accompagnements pour piano peuvent être joués sur différents instruments à clavier. Le clavecin ou l'orgue, ou des sons similaires obtenus sur un clavier électronique, sont adéquats, en particulier pour les morceaux de la Renaissance. Les morceaux les plus anciens, du Moyen Age, nous sont parvenus sous forme de simple ligne mélodique, les accompagnements ont donc été arrangés librement, normalement en se basant sur des ostinati. Mais les mélodies rendront aussi bien si les musiciens y ajoutent leurs propres bourdons et/ou percussions. Pour les mélodies ultérieures, nous savons que les musiciens de la Renaissance aimaient improviser des variations ou « divisions » sur des airs connus. Certaines sont suggérées ici, mais les musiciens sont toujours encouragés à créer les leurs !

Je tiens à remercier John Bryan et le York Early Music Festival, ainsi que Polly Waterfield pour sa perspicacité dans l'enseignement de la musique ancienne et du violon, et Anthony Marks pour avoir fait en sorte que la « tapisserie ne se défasse jamais », et surtout tous les musiciens avec qui j'ai, à différentes périodes, voyagé en Europe avec des housses d'instruments aux formes étranges, jouant du luth, de la viole, du rebec et du violon.

Edward Huws Jones

Notes aux exécutants

English dance Cet air enlevé a quelque chose d'unique – aucun morceau de danse comparable ne nous est parvenu de l'Angleterre médiévale. La première moitié de la mélodie a un motif bien défini, puis elle s'envole, plutôt à la manière d'une improvisation. Si vous désirez en jouer une version plus courte, arrêtez-vous à la mesure 24. On peut trouver une transcription littérale de l'original dans *Historical Anthology of Music* de Davison et Apel (1946).

Estampie royale La plupart des danses médiévales sont de ce type, connu sous le nom d'estampie. Une estampie consiste en une suite de sections courtes. Chacune est jouée deux fois, avec les mêmes dénouements alternés répétés au cours du morceau. Celle-ci provient d'un recueil d'estampies françaises du XIIIème siècle. Ces danses doivent être rapides : écouter l'interprétation endiablée de David Munrow et James Blades dans *Music of the Crusades*.

L'homme armé Cette chanson folklorique française est l'une des plus célèbres de toutes les mélodies médiévales. « Méfiez-vous de l'homme armé : vous aurez besoin d'une armure en fer ! ». L'interprétation doit être bien rythmée et enjouée.

Winder wie ist Neithart von Reuenthal était un « minnesinger », l'équivalent allemand du troubadour. Cette chanson célèbre la venue du mois de mai et la fin de l'hiver. La mélodie est normalement jouée dans une mesure à quatre temps, mais cette version en 6/8 fait ressortir son côté enjoué.

Saltarello   Ce morceau provient d'un manuscrit italien du XIV^(ème) siècle, conservé à la British Library à Londres. *Saltarello* convient tout à fait au violon folklorique, avec ses accords de quinte et son irrépressible rythme de gigue.

J'ay mis mon cuer   Les paroles sont peut-être d'une chanson d'amour, mais la musique doit être assurée et rythmée. Notre version ne se sert que de la première moitié de la chanson originale à trois voix de Dufay. La partie de clavier se base assez librement sur les deux voix inférieures. Des interprétations enthousiastes de ce morceau et du suivant figurent dans *Dufay : Chansons* de l'Ensemble Unicorn.

Pour le regard de vos beaux yeux   Il s'agit de l'une des œuvres les plus populaires de Dufay, on la trouve dans pas moins de quatorze manuscrits contemporains. Les paroles se passent de commentaire. L'interprétation doit être tendre et lyrique. Les deux parties inférieures sont attribuées au deuxième violon et au violon d'accompagnement, trois violons peuvent donc jouer cette œuvre dans sa forme originale.

Pastime with good company   Le roi Henry VIII d'Angleterre était un fervent musicien amateur. Cette mélodie et la suivante proviennent d'un manuscrit compilé à la cour au début de son règne. Ce morceau gagne à être ornementé et peut être embelli de nombreuses manières selon l'imagination et la technique des interprètes.

Hélas madame   Ceci est également une chanson de la cour du roi Henry VIII. Les paroles, en français, sont plutôt plaintives mais la musique est pleine d'ardeur et exubérante !

Recercada   Diego Ortiz était un joueur de viole espagnol et son *Tratado de Glosas* (1553) était une sorte de méthode pour apprendre seul à composer des divisions (variations ornementales). Recercada veut dire recherche, exploration des possibilités d'un thème ou d'une idée musicale. Cette recercada est assez ludique, presque comme un délicieux gribouillage musical. Vous aimerez les syncopes des blanches et des noires pointées.

Ach Els'lein, liebstes Elselein   Cette chanson folklorique poignante était fort appréciée par les compositeurs allemands de la Renaissance. Cet arrangement prend comme point de départ la version publiée dans le *Glogauer Liederbuch*.

La gamba   Cette mélodie et ses harmonies furent le thème de nombreuses divisions, Ortiz donne deux versions différentes. En Angleterre, on lui a même ajouté des paroles de Sir Thomas Wyatt : « Blame not my lute » (« N'accusez point mon luth »).

Calata   Ce morceau a toujours été l'un de mes airs favoris, il a toute la spontanéité de la musique folklorique authentique. La mélodie, avec son rythme guilleret, presque arrogant, est adaptée d'une tablature pour luth du XVI^(ème) siècle.

Kemp's jig   J'ai appris cet air grâce à un enregistrement fait par Gryphon, un groupe folk-rock des années 1970. Cette version est tirée d'une tablature anglaise pour luth du XVI^(ème) siècle. C'est un air de danse typique de la période élisabéthaine avec un rythme exubérant à deux temps.

Watkins' ale   Cette mélodie délicieuse et plutôt espiègle et ses variations sont adaptées de versions figurant dans le *Fitzwilliam Virginal Book* et le *Welde Lute Book*. Les variations sont à discrétion - si vous le préférez, répétez simplement les lignes 1, 3 et 5.

Ronde : Pour quoy   Susato était moins un compositeur qu'un arrangeur et un éditeur. Dans ses danses à quatre voix l'instrumentation n'est pas indiquée, mais cette gracieuse mélodie convient parfaitement au violon. Dans tous ces morceaux de danses, il est important de varier le phrasé : il est recommandé de jouer les passages conjoints plutôt legato, et les intervalles plus importants et les notes répétées de manière plus détachée.

La morisque   Nous avons là un air de danse folklorique anglais simple et vivace au rythme joyeux.

Pavane : La Vénissienne   Ce morceau est écrit sur une basse extrêmement populaire connue sous le nom de passamezzo antico, la même basse en fait que l'on trouve dans *Greensleeves*. La pavane est solennelle, majestueuse mais pas trop lente.

La bouree   *Terpsichore* de Praetorius (1612) est une vaste anthologie de musique de danse dont la plus grande partie date du siècle précédent. *La Bouree* doit être jouée sur un rythme solide à deux temps pour faire ressortir des motifs rythmiques plutôt comiques.

Gaillarde : Mrs Winter's jump   Praetorius intitule ceci simplement *Gaillarde* mais il s'agit en fait d'un arrangement d'une mélodie populaire élisabéthaine. Le titre (« Le saut de madame Winter ») nous indique exactement comment la jouer !

Vorwort

Die vorliegende Sammlung umspannt vier Jahrhunderte und mehr als fünf Länder und enthält einige besonders schöne Stücke aus der Schatztruhe früher abendländischer Musik.

Die Alte Musik fesselt mich schon seit den 70er Jahren, in denen Musiker wie David Munrow und Anthony Rooley ganze Welten mittelalterlicher und Renaissance-Musik wiederentdeckten und in Aufführungen zu neuem Leben erweckten. Heute präsentieren z.B. Jan Garbarek und das Hilliard-Ensemble einem weltweiten Publikum eine Mischung aus früher Mehrstimmigkeit und Jazz, und CDs mit gregorianischen Gesängen oder Stücken von Hildegard von Bingen stehen oben in den Hitparaden. Die Alte Musik ist aus ihrem Elfenbeinturm herausgetreten und gehört mittlerweile zur Alltagskultur.

Die Violine zählt nicht wirklich zum Instrumentarium der Alten Musik, aber sie entwickelte sich bereits kurz nach 1500, also in der Frühzeit der Renaissance, mehr oder weniger zu der Form, in der wir sie heute kennen. Die meisten Stücke in dieser Sammlung haben einen Bezug zu Saiteninstrumenten, entweder zur Violine selbst oder zu ihren Vorläufern wie Rebec, mittelalterliche Fiedel oder Viole. Tatsächlich passen alle Stücke hervorragend zur Violine, und natürlich sind Spielfreude und Begeisterung des Spielers hier wichtiger als notengetreue historische Genauigkeit!

Die Bearbeitungen dieser Sammlung sind demselben flexiblen Ansatz wie die anderen Bände dieser Serie verpflichtet und können als Solo-Stücke, Duette, Trios oder in größerer Besetzung gespielt werden. Violinbegleitungen für fortgeschrittenere Spieler stehen am Ende des Bandes. Die Klavierbegleitung kann auf verschiedenen Tasteninstrumenten gespielt werden. Cembalo oder Orgel – oder vergleichbare Klangfarben auf einem elektronischen Keyboard – passen gut, besonders bei den Renaissance-Stücken. Alle frühen mittelalterlichen Stücke sind nur in einstimmiger Form überliefert, so dass es sich bei den Begleitungen um freie Bearbeitungen handelt, die in der Regel auf einem Ostinato basieren. Aber die Spieler können auch selbst zu den Melodien eine passende Bass- und/oder Schlagzeug-Begleitung hinzufügen. Bei den Renaissance-Stücken wissen wir, dass damals mit Vorliebe Variationen über bekannte Melodien improvisiert wurden. Einige davon sind hier aufgenommen, aber die Ausführenden seien ausdrücklich zu eigenen Erfindungen ermuntert!

Mein Dank geht an John Bryan und das Early Music Festival in York; an Polly Waterfield für ihre hilfreichen Einblicke sowohl in die Alte Musik als auch in die Violinpädagogik; an Anthony Marks, der mich bei der richtigen Auswahl aus der Schatztruhe unterstützte; und vor allem an alle Musiker, mit denen ich mehrfach mit seltsam geformten Instrumenten-kästen durch Europa gereist bin, um Laute, Viole, Rebec und Fiedel zu spielen.

Edward Huws Jones

Anmerkungen zur Ausfuhrung

Englischer Tanz Diese mitreißende Melodie ist ein Unikat – aus dem mittelalterlichen England ist uns keine vergleichbare Tanzmusik erhalten. Die erste Hälfte der Melodie weist eine klare Form auf, die sich dann beinahe in eine Art Improvisation auflöst. Falls Sie eine kürzere Version spielen möchten, können Sie bei Takt 24 aufhören. Eine genaue Transkription des Originals findet sich bei Davison und Apel, *Historical Anthology of Music* (1946).

Estampie royale Die meisten mittelalterlichen Tänze gehörten zum Typus der Estampie oder Estampida, die jeweils aus einer Reihe kurzer Abschnitte bestanden. Jeder wird zweimal gespielt, wobei die gleichen, alternierenden Schlüsse das ganze Stück hindurch wiederholt werden. Der vorliegende Tanz stammt aus einer Sammlung französischer Estampies aus dem 13. Jahrhundert. Diese Tänze fordern ein rasantes Tempo: Hören Sie sich als Beispiel die mitreißende Interpretation von David Munrow und James Blades auf *Music of the Crusades* an.

L'homme armé Dieses französische Volkslied gehört zu den berühmtesten mittelalterlichen Melodien. Der Text bedeutet ungefähr: "Hab acht vor dem bewaffneten Mann: du wird eine eiserne Rüstung brauchen!" Der Vortrag sollte entsprechend rhythmisch und ausgelassen sein.

Winder wie ist Neithart von Reuenthal (13. Jhdt.) war ein Minnesänger aus Bayern. Dieses Lied feiert das Kommen des Monats Mai und das Ende des Winters. Die Melodie wird meist im Viervierteltakt angegeben, doch betont diese Sechsachtel-Version ihren lebhaft schwingenden Rhythmus.

Saltarello Dieses Stück stammt aus einem im 14. Jahrhundert verfassten italienischen Manuskript, das sich heute in der British Library in London befindet. Der *Saltarello* hat echte Volksmusik-Qualitäten mit seinen offenen Quinten und unbezähmbaren gigue-artigen Rhythmen.

J'ay mis mon cuer Der Text mag zwar von Liebe handeln, doch muss die Musik vor allem resolut und rhythmisch kraftvoll klingen. Unsere Fassung enthält nur die erste Hälfte von Dufays ursprünglich dreiteiligem Lied. Die Klavierstimme basiert lose auf den beiden unteren Stimmen. Anregende Darbietungen dieses und des folgenden Stücks sind auf der Einspielung *Dufay: Chansons* des Ensemble Unicorn zu hören.

Pour le regard de vos beaux yeux Dies war eines von Dufays beliebtesten Werken – es findet sich in immerhin 14 zeitgenössischen Manuskripten. Die Worte sagen alles: "Beim Anblick ihrer schönen Augen . . .". Die Darbietung sollte entsprechend zart und lyrisch sein. Die beiden unteren Stimmen Dufays sind in die zweite Geige und in die Violinbegleitung übernommen, so dass drei Geigen das Stück in der Originalversion spielen können.

Pastime with good company Heinrich VIII. von England war ein begeisterter Musikliebhaber. Diese und die folgende Melodie stammen aus einem Manuskript, das an seinem Hof zu Beginn seiner Regentschaft zusammengetragen wurde. Das Stück eignet sich für das Spiel mit Verzierungen und kann je nach Fähigkeiten und Fantasie der Spieler entsprechend ausgeschmückt werden.

Hélas madame Noch ein Lied vom Hofe Heinrichs VIII. Der französische Text ist zwar recht wehmütig, doch die Musik selbst ist temperamentvoll und ausgelassen!

Recercada Diego Ortiz war ein spanischer Violaspieler, dessen *Tratado de Glosas* (1553) ein Lehrbuch für das Musizieren und Variieren war. Recercada (Ricercar) bedeutet auf die Suche gehen – die Möglichkeiten eines musikalischen Themas oder Motivs erforschen. Diese Recercada hat einen spielerischen Charakter und gleicht einer hübschen musikalischen Skizze. Besonders ansprechend: die synkopierten halben Noten und die punktierten Viertelnoten.

Ach Els'lein, liebstes Elselein Dieses prägnante Volkslied war bei deutschen Komponisten der Renaissance äußerst beliebt. Die vorliegende Fassung basiert auf der Version im *Glogauer Liederbuch*.

La gamba Diese Melodie und die ihr zugrundeliegende Akkordsequenz wurden oft als Material für Variationen verwendet – Ortiz gibt zwei unterschiedliche Versionen an. In England hat sie Sir Thomas Wyatt sogar textiert: "Blame not my Lute".

Calata Dies ist seit jeher eine meiner Lieblingsmelodien; sie zeichnet sich durch die phantasievolle Spontaneität echter Volksmusik aus. Die Melodie mit ihrem spritzigen, beinahe stolzierenden Rhythmus wurde hier nach einer Lauten-tabulatur des 16. Jahrhunderts bearbeitet.

Kemp's jig Dieser Melodie begegnete ich erstmals in den siebziger Jahren auf einer Platte der englischen Folk-Rock-Gruppe Gryphon. Die vorliegende Version basiert auf einer englischen Lautentabulatur aus dem 16. Jahrhundert. Sie ist eine typische elisabethanische Tanzmelodie mit einem ausgelassenen Zweierrhythmus.

Watkins' ale Diese reizende, ziemlich freche Melodie und ihre Begleitvariationen sind Bearbeitungen aus dem *Fitzwilliam Virginal Book* und dem *Welde Lute Book*. Die Variationen sind optional: Sie können auch einfach nur Zeile 1, 3 und 5 wiederholen.

Ronde: Pour quoy Susato war eigentlich kein Komponist, sondern Bearbeiter und Verleger. Seine vierstimmigen Tänze geben keine bestimmte Besetzung an, doch ist diese graziöse Melodie ideal für die Geige geeignet. Bei all diesen Tanzstücken kommt es darauf an, die Artikulation zu wechseln: oft ist es sinnvoll, die stufenweise melodische Bewegung ziemlich gebunden zu spielen, während größere Intervalle oder Tonwiederholungen eher voneinander abgesetzt gespielt werden sollten.

La morisque Dies ist eine lebhafte, unkomplizierte Moresca-Tanzmelodie in übermütigem Zweiertakt.

Pavane: La Venissienne Grundlage dieses Stücks ist die sehr beliebte Basslinie *Passamezzo antico*, derselbe Bass wie in *Greensleeves*. Die Pavane zeichnet sich durch ein prozessionsartiges Gepräge aus, würdevoll, aber nicht schleppend.

La bouree Praetorius' *Terpsichore* (1612) ist eine umfangreiche Sammlung von Tänzen, die meist bis in das davorliegende Jahrhundert zurückreichen. *La Bouree* benötigt einen kräftigen Zweierpuls, damit die recht komischen rhythmischen Motive deutlich herauskommen.

Gaillarde: Mrs Winter's jump Praetorius nannte dieses Stück einfach *Gaillarde*, doch ist es eigentlich die Bearbeitung einer beliebten elisabethanischen Melodie. Der Titel "Frau Winters Sprung" weist schon darauf hin, wie dieses Stück gespielt werden soll!

English dance

Estampie royale

13th century French

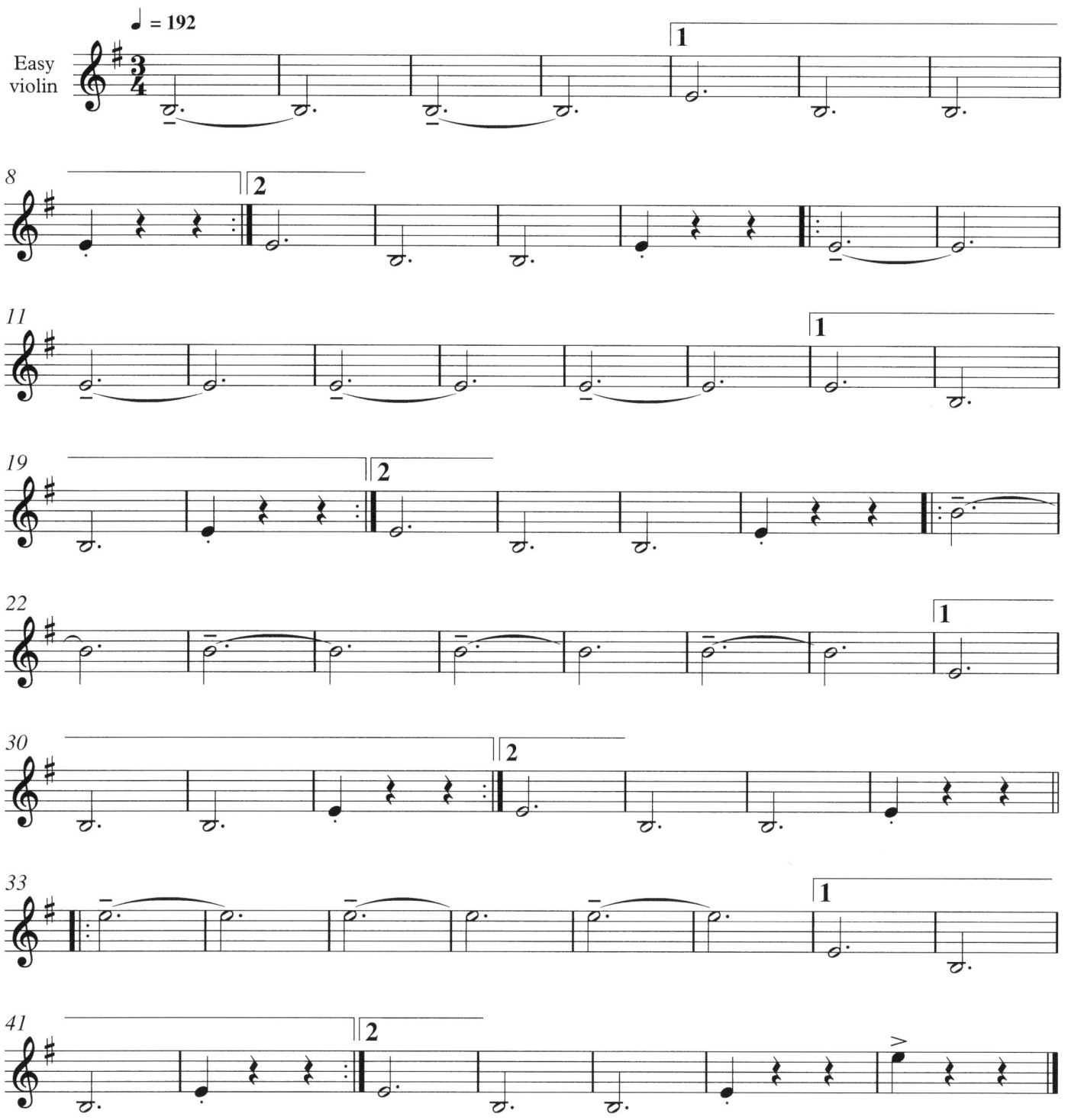

L'homme armé

15th century French

© Copyright 2000 by Boosey & Hawkes Music Publishers Ltd

Winder wie ist

Neithart von Reuenthal
(early 13th century)

Saltarello

14th century Italian

J'ay mis mon cuer

Guillaume Dufay
(d.1474)

Par le regard de vos beaux yeux

Guillaume Dufay
(d.1474)

This part follows Dufay's original contratenor line (see note)

© Copyright 2000 by Boosey & Hawkes Music Publishers Ltd

Pastime with good company

attrib. Henry VIII
(1491–1547)

Suggested divisions for second verse (EHJ)

© Copyright 2000 by Boosey & Hawkes Music Publishers Ltd

Hélas madame

attrib. Henry VIII
(1491–1547)

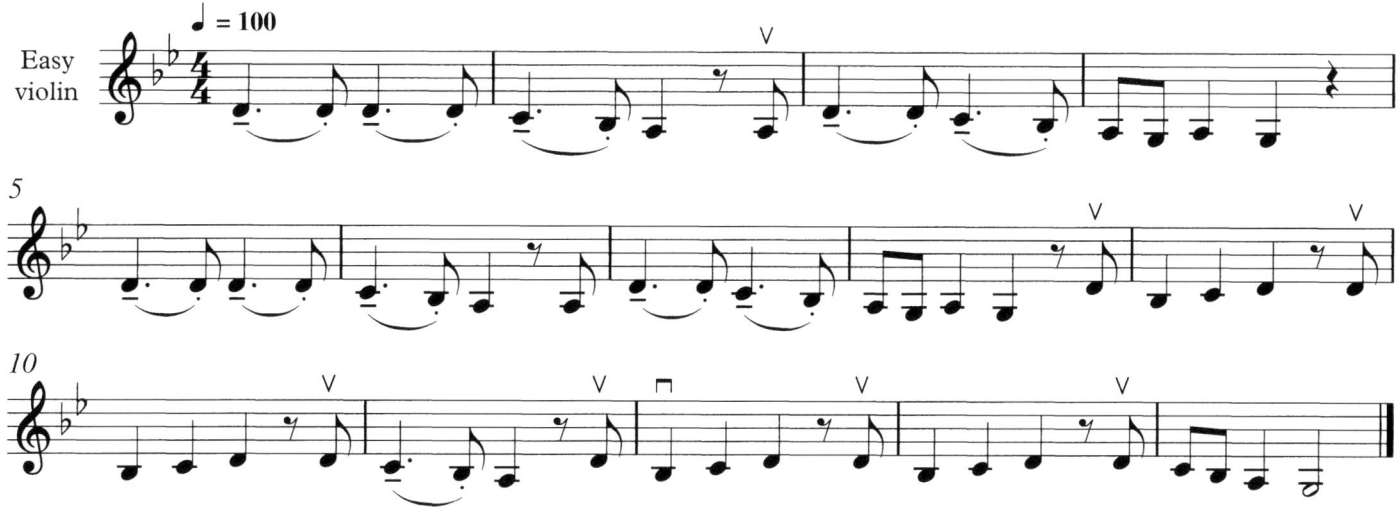

Recercada

Diego Ortiz, 'Tratado de Glosas' 1553

© Copyright 2000 by Boosey & Hawkes Music Publishers Ltd

Ach Els'lein, liebstes Elselein

15th century German

La gamba

16th century Italian

Calata

16th century Italian

Kemp's jig

16th century English

© Copyright 2000 by Boosey & Hawkes Music Publishers Ltd

Watkins' ale

16th century English

Ronde: Pour quoy

Tielman Susato, 'Dansereye' 1551

La morisque

Tielman Susato, 'Dansereye' 1551

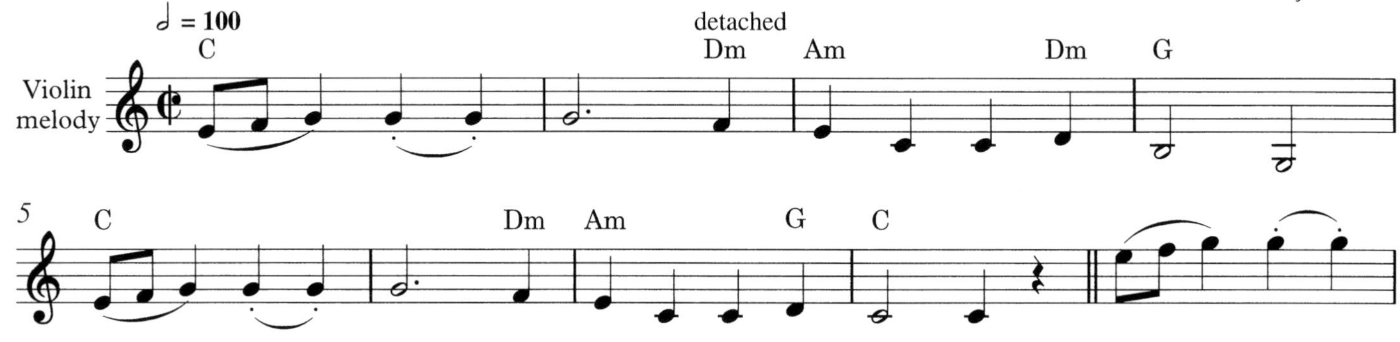

Pavane: La Venissienne

Claude Gervaise, 'Quart Livre de Danseries' 1550

* *Suggested additional divisions* (EHJ)

© Copyright 2000 by Boosey & Hawkes Music Publishers Ltd

La bouree

Michael Praetorius, 'Terpsichore' 1612

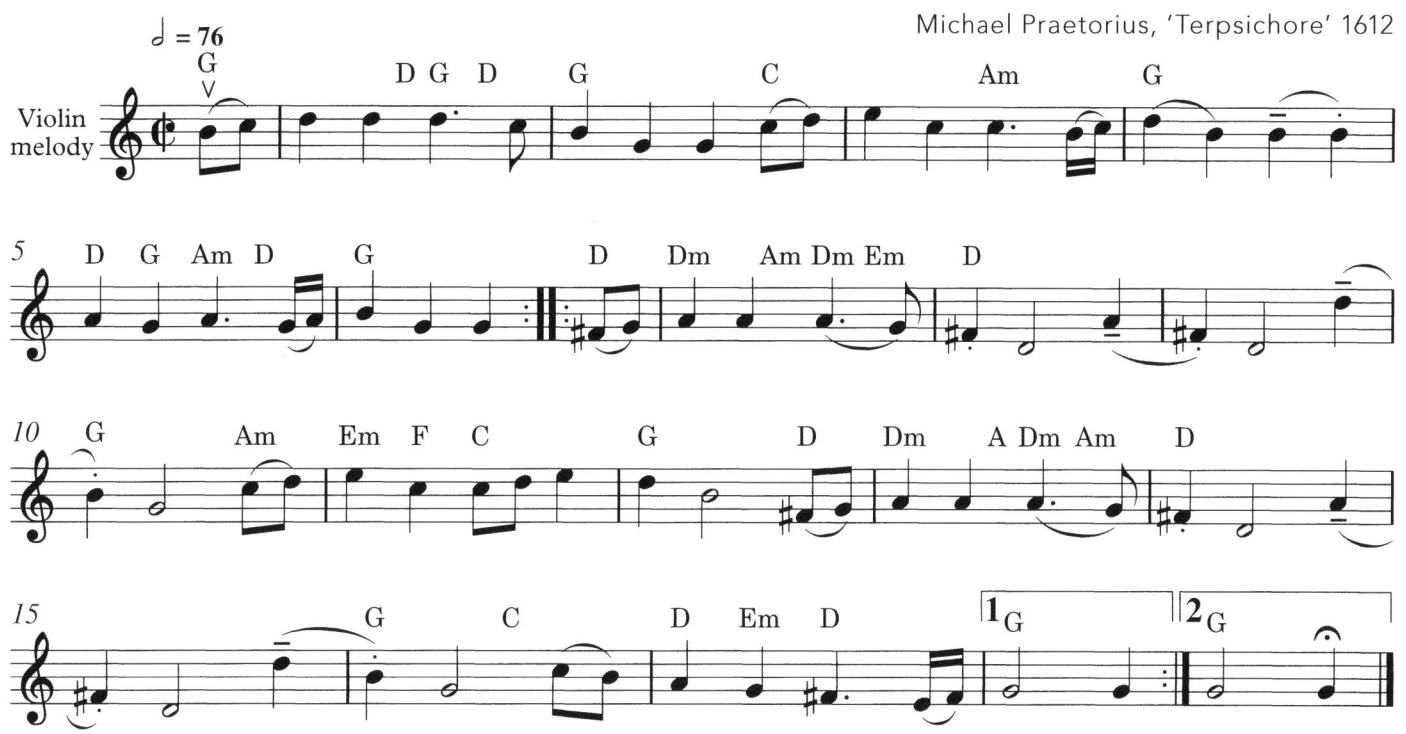

© Copyright 2000 by Boosey & Hawkes Music Publishers Ltd

Gaillarde: Mrs Winter's jump

Michael Praetorius, 'Terpsichore' 1612

© Copyright 2000 by Boosey & Hawkes Music Publishers Ltd

PIANO/VIOLIN ACCOMPANIMENT

Traditional fiddle music from around the world

EARLY MUSIC FIDDLER

Selected and arranged by
Edward Huws Jones

BOOSEY & HAWKES

Published by Boosey & Hawkes Music Publishers Ltd
Aldwych House
71–91 Aldwych
London
WC2B 4HN

www.boosey.com

© Copyright 2000 by Boosey & Hawkes Music Publishers Ltd
New edition © Copyright 2024 by Boosey & Hawkes Music Publishers Ltd

ISMN 979-0-060-11217-1 | ISBN 978-0-85162-277-4 (complete)
ISMN 979-0-060-11218-8 | ISBN 978-0-85162-278-1 (separately sold violin part)

Printed by Halstan:
Halstan UK, 2-10 Plantation Road, Amersham, Bucks, HP6 6HJ. United Kingdom
Halstan DE, Weißliliengasse 4, 55116 Mainz. Germany

Music setting by Jack Thompson

Cover design by Chloë Alexander Design
Cover image: Paul Hughes

EARLY MUSIC FIDDLER

Selected and arranged by
Edward Huws Jones

		piano score	violin accompaniment

MEDIEVAL SONGS AND DANCES

English dance	*13th century English*	2	47
Estampie royale	*13th century French*	6	48
L'homme armé	*15th century French*	10	49
Winder wie ist	*Neithart von Reuenthal*	12	49
Saltarello	*14th century Italian*	14	50

MUSIC AT COURT

J'ay mis mon cuer	*Guillaume Dufay*	17	51
Par le regard de vos beaux yeux	*Guillaume Dufay*	18	51
Pastime with good company	*atrrib. Henry VIII*	20	52
Hélas madame	*atrrib. Henry VIII*	22	52
Recercada	*Diego Ortiz*	24	53

RENAISSANCE POPULAR MUSIC

Ach Els'lein, liebstes Elselein	*15th century German*	28	54
La gamba	*16th century Italian*	29	54
Calata	*16th century Italian*	32	54
Kemp's jig	*16th century English*	34	55
Watkins' ale	*16th century English*	36	56

THE RENAISSANCE DANCE-BAND

Ronde: Pour quoy	*Tielman Susato*	38	56
La morisque	*Tielman Susato*	40	56
Pavane: La Venissienne	*Claude Gervaise*	42	57
La bouree	*Michael Praetorius*	44	58
Gaillarde: Mrs Winter's jump	*Michael Praetorius*	46	58

English dance

13th century English

4

Estampie royale

13th century French

L'homme armé

15th century French

Winder wie ist

Neithart von Reuenthal
(early 13th century)

Saltarello

14th century Italian

J'ay mis mon cuer

Guillaume Dufay
(d.1474)

Par le regard de vos beaux yeux

Guillaume Dufay
(d.1474)

Pastime with good company

attrib. Henry VIII
(1491–1547)

Suggested divisions for second verse (EHJ)

Hélas madame

attrib. Henry VIII
(1491–1547)

Recercada

Diego Ortiz, 'Tratado de Glosas' 1553

© Copyright 2000 by Boosey & Hawkes Music Publishers Ltd

Ach Els'lein, liebstes Elselein

15th century German

La gamba

16th century Italian

© Copyright 2000 by Boosey & Hawkes Music Publishers Ltd

Suggested divisions for second verse (EHJ)

Calata

16th century Italian

© Copyright 2000 by Boosey & Hawkes Music Publishers Ltd

Kemp's jig

16th century English

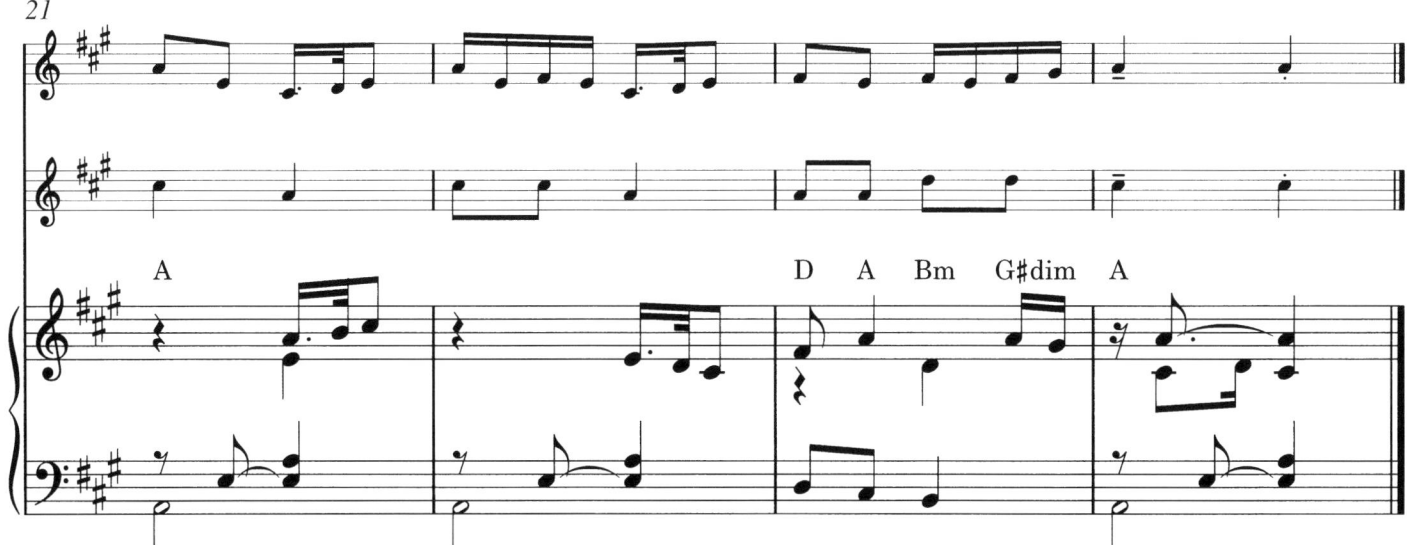

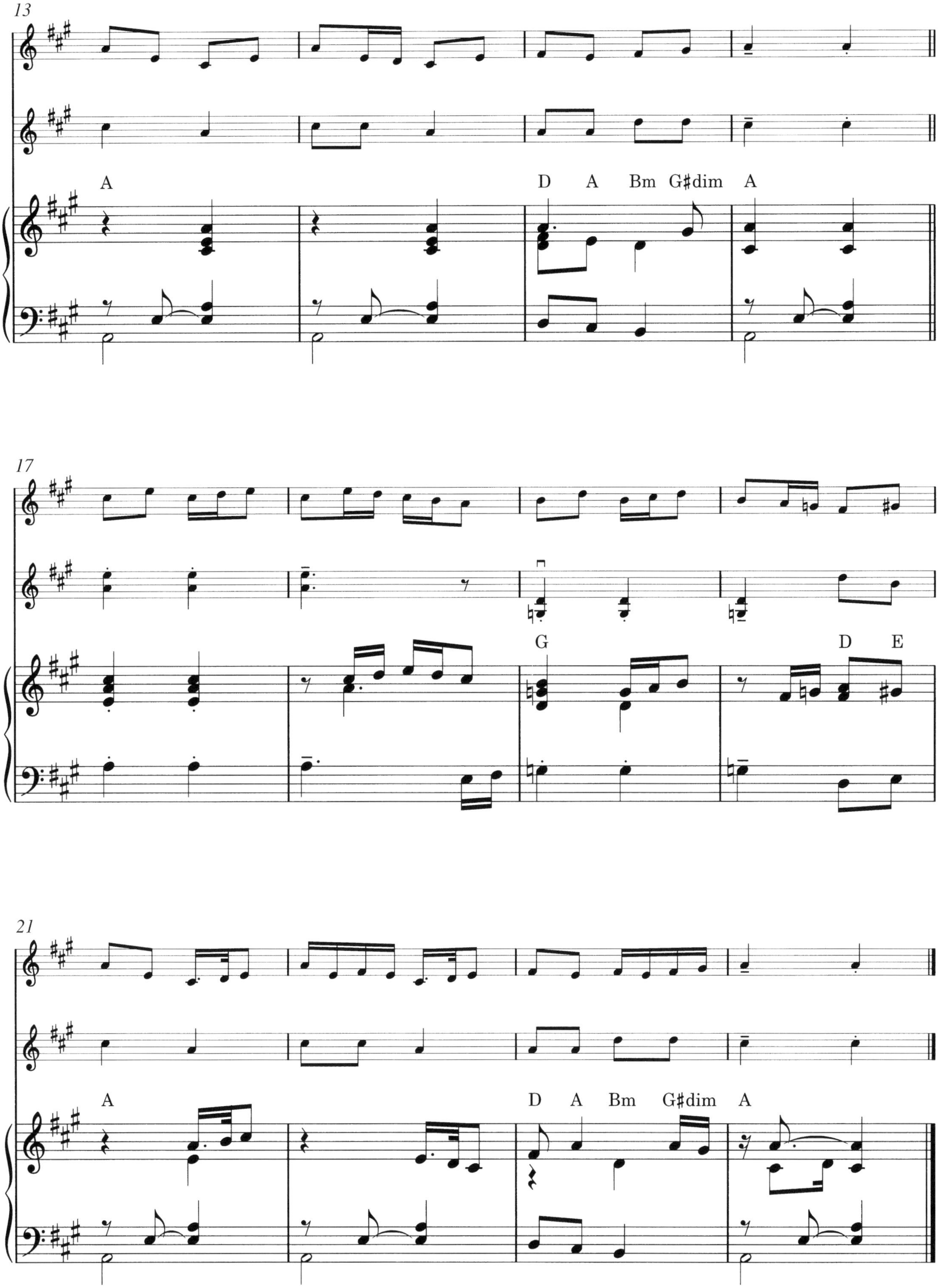
13
A
D A Bm G♯dim A
17
G
D E
21
A
D A Bm G♯dim A

Watkins' ale

16th century English

© Copyright 2000 by Boosey & Hawkes Music Publishers Ltd

Ronde: Pour quoy

Tielman Susato, 'Dansereye' 1551

© Copyright 2000 by Boosey & Hawkes Music Publishers Ltd

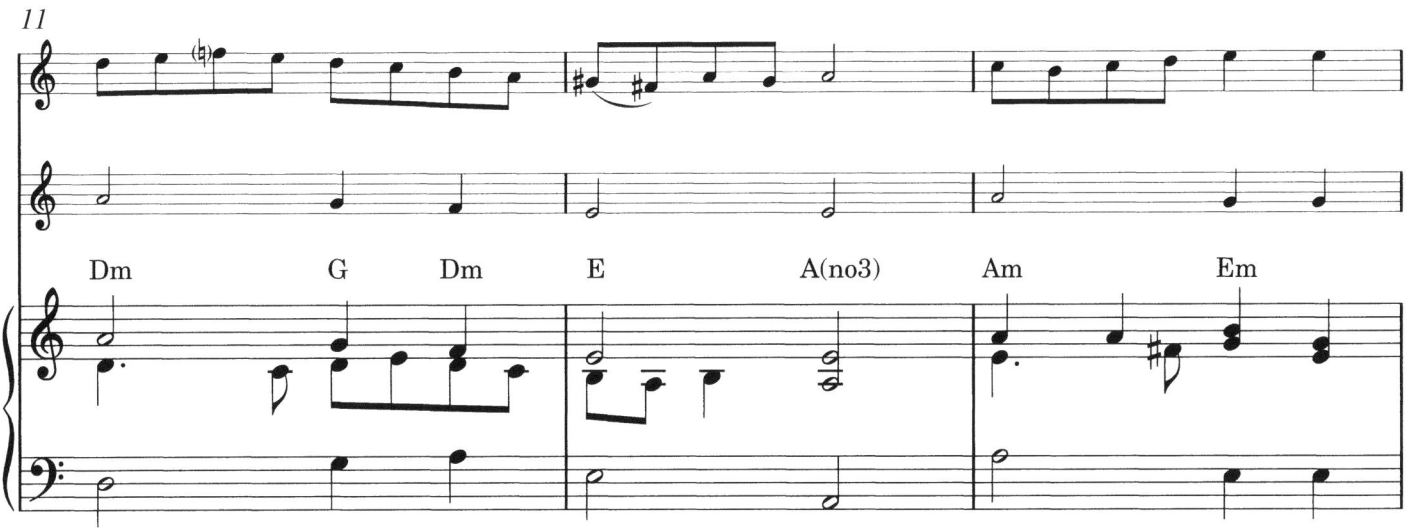

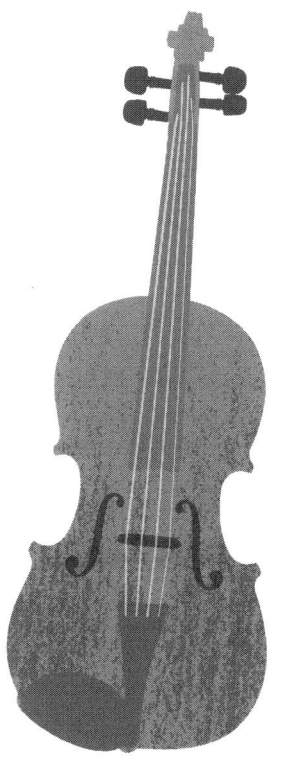

La morisque

Tielman Susato, 'Dansereye' 1551

Pavane: La Venissienne

Claude Gervaise, 'Quart Livre de Danseries' 1550

* *Suggested additional divisions (EHJ)*

© Copyright 2000 by Boosey & Hawkes Music Publishers Ltd

La bouree

Michael Praetorius, 'Terpsichore' 1612

Gaillarde: Mrs Winter's jump

Michael Praetorius, 'Terpsichore' 1612

VIOLIN ACCOMPANIMENT

English dance

13th century English

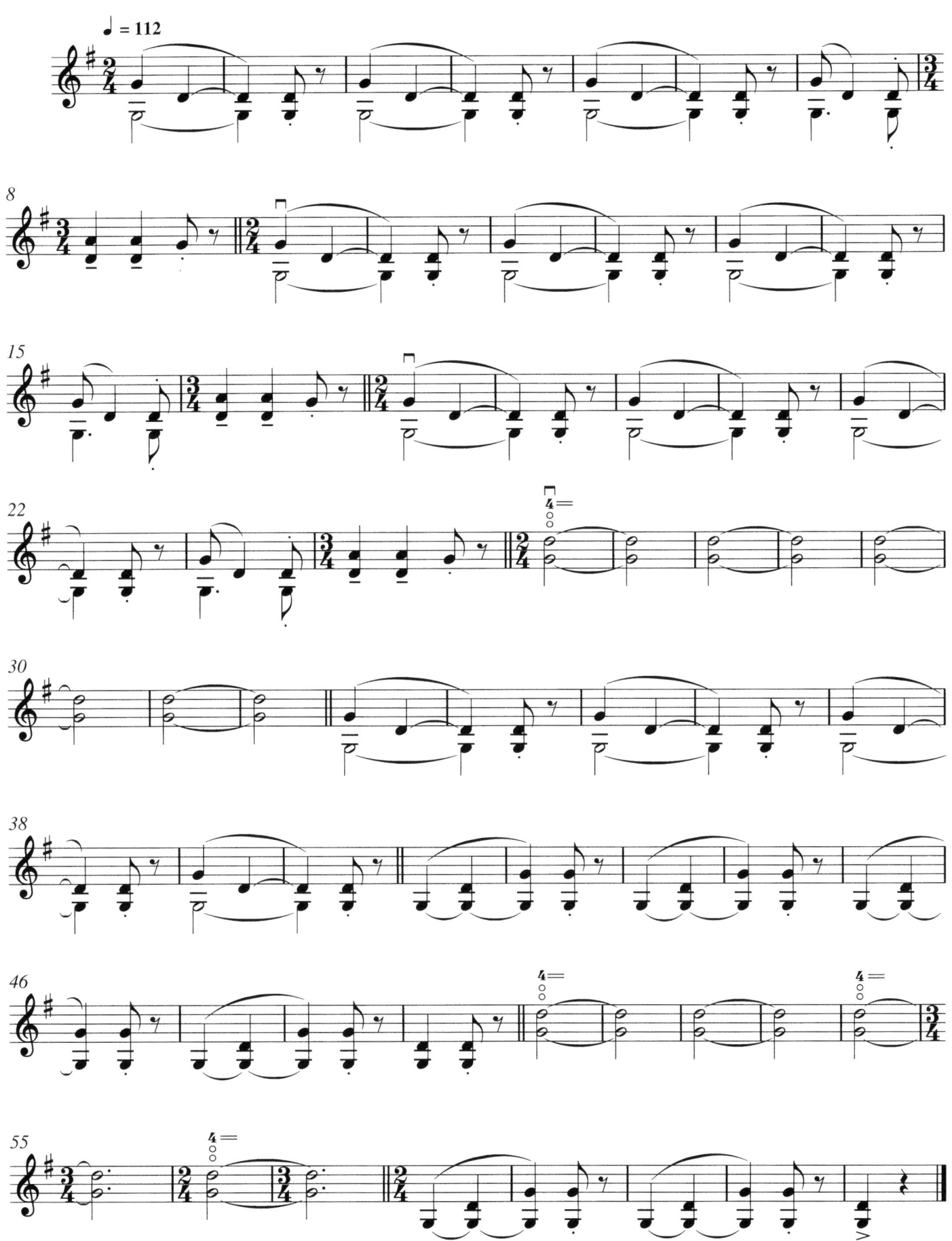

© Copyright 2000 by Boosey & Hawkes Music Publishers Ltd

Estampie royale

VIOLIN ACCOMPANIMENT

13th century French

© Copyright 2000 by Boosey & Hawkes Music Publishers Ltd

VIOLIN ACCOMPANIMENT

L'homme armé

15th century French

© Copyright 2000 by Boosey & Hawkes Music Publishers Ltd

Winder wie ist

Neithart von Reuenthal
(early 13th century)

© Copyright 2000 by Boosey & Hawkes Music Publishers Ltd

Saltarello

VIOLIN ACCOMPANIMENT

14th century Italian

© Copyright 2000 by Boosey & Hawkes Music Publishers Ltd

Violin Accompaniment

J'ay mis mon cuer

Guillaume Dufay
(d.1474)

© Copyright 2000 by Boosey & Hawkes Music Publishers Ltd

Par le regard de vos beaux yeux

Guillaume Dufay
(d.1474)

This part follows Dufay's original tenor line (see note)

© Copyright 2000 by Boosey & Hawkes Music Publishers Ltd

Pastime with good company

attrib. Henry VIII
(1491–1547)

Hélas madame

attrib. Henry VIII
(1491–1547)

VIOLIN ACCOMPANIMENT

Recercada

Diego Ortiz, 'Tratado de Glosas' 1553

© Copyright 2000 by Boosey & Hawkes Music Publishers Ltd

Ach Els'lein, liebstes Elselein

15th century German

© Copyright 2000 by Boosey & Hawkes Music Publishers Ltd

La gamba

16th century Italian

© Copyright 2000 by Boosey & Hawkes Music Publishers Ltd

Calata

16th century Italian

© Copyright 2000 by Boosey & Hawkes Music Publishers Ltd

Kemp's jig

16th century English

Watkins' ale

16th century English

Ronde: Pour quoy

Tielman Susato, 'Dansereye' 1551

La morisque

Tielman Susato, 'Dansereye' 1551

Violin Accompaniment

Pavane: La Venissienne

Claude Gervaise, 'Quart Livre de Danseries' 1550

© Copyright 2000 by Boosey & Hawkes Music Publishers Ltd

VIOLIN ACCOMPANIMENT

La bouree

Michael Praetorius, 'Terpsichore' 1612

© Copyright 2000 by Boosey & Hawkes Music Publishers Ltd

Gaillarde: Mrs Winter's jump

Michael Praetorius, 'Terpsichore' 1612

© Copyright 2000 by Boosey & Hawkes Music Publishers Ltd